ripples FOR reflection

weekly inspirations for unleashing your best self

ripples
FOR reflection

weekly inspirations for
unleashing your best self

Paul Wesselmann
edited by Jamie Markle

For all the Ripplers ...

the ones who help us find upbeat quotes;
the ones who reach out when an issue resonates;
and the ones who extend ripples
out into their communities

... this is for you.

Contents

Preface	8
How to Read This Book	10

Winter — 12

Meaning	14
Becoming You	16
Thriving in the Mess	18
The Power to Choose	20
Embracing Wholeness	22
Love's Shine	24
Healing from Hurts	26
Letting Go	28
The Journey of Un-Becoming	30
Being Tender	32
Mini-Puzzles	34
Finding & Unfurling Joy	36
Allowing Others In	38

Spring — 40

Spring Blossoms	42
Celebrating Struggle	44
Ripples of Kindness	46
Knowing Yourself	48
Comparison Hangover	50
Quirky You	52
The Tensions and the Doldrums	54
Your Reason, Your Dance	56
Throwing Back	58
Common Enchantment	60
Trust Your Power	62
Let Yourself In	64
Slight Adjustments	66

Summer	**68**
Rut Departure	70
Little Choices	72
Museum of Beautiful Stuff	74
Refracting Peace	76
Risk Being Seen	78
Learning to Surf	80
Delusions of Disconnection	82
Becoming Quiet	84
Pain vs. Suffering	86
Here, Now	88
Helper's High	90
The Hero Within	92
Imperfectionism	94
Autumn	**96**
Light & Love	98
Liking Living	100
The Greatness of Your Smallness	102
Scare Your Fears	104
The Evolution of Happiness	106
Ripples of Experimentation	108
Squeeze and Release	110
The Magic of Words	112
Crazy Powerful	114
The Freedom of Forgiveness	116
Enoughness	118
Bubbling Brooks	120
Whimsical Graces	122
Thanks	124
About the Author	127

Preface

"Remember there's no such thing as a small act of kindness. Every act creates a ripple with no logical end."

—SCOTT ADAMS

Like many worthwhile adventures, Ripples began with a small idea.

Seeking an inspirational finale for presentations that were part of his work as a trainer and keynote speaker, Paul developed a simple quote-sharing activity by printing out a few dozen upbeat quotes onto small cards and distributing one to each person with the instruction: "You're about to get a quote that has meaning for something going on in your life right now."

The quote exercise was a BIG HIT and helped people to think about what was going on in their lives and connect with others. Many people reported holding on to (and even carrying around) the quote for months, even years. This led to the idea of zooming out a brief email on Monday mornings with a couple of powerful quotes and something to ponder for the week so each of us could bring our best selves to school, work, and life.

Paul called the emails RIPPLES as a reminder of the ongoing impact that even our tiniest actions have on the world around us.

What began in 1999 as a few dozen people responding positively to these weekly splashes evolved into a vibrant community with thousands of like-minded souls who participate actively by providing a steady stream of quote submissions and sharing their favorite topics with friends and family as well as colleagues and classmates.

In the summer of 2018, these small splashes of inspiration celebrated a big milestone when the 1,000th issue of Ripples zoomed out to more than 30,000 subscribers and was read by many more on social media. The idea for this book was born after receiving numerous requests from Ripplers for a way that Ripples could live not only in their inboxes but also on their bookshelves.

Jamie brought his background in the publishing industry to the task of sifting through all 1,000+ issues to assemble this collection of 52 Ripples—one for each week of the year. With many topics to choose from, he created a collection of Ripples that captures the ups and downs of life, keeping in mind how small acts can make big impacts over time. Short or long, funny or poignant, it is our hope that the reader discovers some ideas on how to meet life head on and move forward in times of joy AND adversity.

It has been an amazing adventure for us to work on this project together, and we are delighted to arrive at the place in our journey where this book of selected Ripples is in your hands. May it unleash ripples of encouragement, connection, joy, and peace.

Paul + Jamie

How to Read This Book

However you want!

Ripples was created as an email to deliver a weekly splash of inspiration intended to take one minute or less to read. Each Ripples email followed a simple format:

Pebble: a brief quote or saying
Boulder: a longer passage, song lyric, or poem
Ponder: a few paragraphs that unpack the theme

We wanted to give you, the reader of this book, a similar experience, so we gathered 52 of our favorite Ripples—one for each week of the year—and arranged them into four sections, one for each season.

The beauty of a printed book is that you have a year's worth of Ripples at your fingertips. And the best part of this compilation is that YOU get to choose when and how you read Ripples. Depending on your mood, you could:

- Start at the beginning and read one Ripple each week
- Skim the book, looking for themes and quotes that grab your attention
- Scan the Contents page and see if there is a topic that calls to you
- Flip open the book to a random page and let the universe decide what inspiration might be helpful for you
- Search for a specific theme that addresses a particular concern you're facing
- Or, any combination of these approaches as your journey progresses!

To help you navigate the book, we classified each issue into one of five major themes. We thought it would be useful to identify the themes with icons to serve as guideposts when you're seeking inspiration to face a specific challenge:

- **Grow:** there is always another step to take, another lesson to learn
- **Shine:** the world wants you to recognize and unleash your awesomeness
- **Enjoy:** there is fun to experience, excitement to share, and gratitude to savor
- **Connect:** building bridges with the people you encounter in work, school, and life
- **Persist:** encouragement to hang in there when facing life's inevitable challenges

If you're trying to pump yourself up you might keep an eye out for the Shine icon; if you are having a tough day then turning to one of the Persist issues might help.

How you use this book is completely up to you—it doesn't really matter your approach as long as you find the inspiration you need to bring your best self to each and every week.

Enjoy the book!

"Welcome, winter. Your late dawns and chilled breath make me lazy, but I love you nonetheless."

—TERRI GUILLEMETS

winter

RIPPLES NUMBER 870

Meaning

PEBBLE

"Most humans feel the transcendent temptation, the emotional drive to festoon the universe with large-scale meaning."

—PAUL KURTZ, SHARED BY RYAN IN ARLINGTON, TX

BOULDER

"Every experience that we have contains purpose and meaning. Each event, each person in our lives embodies an energetic fragment of our own psyche and soul."

—CAROLINE MYSS, SHARED BY PETE IN SEDONA, AZ

PONDER

Each week as I sit down to prepare the next issue of Ripples, my intention is to assemble a 60-second splash of inspiration that elevates the spirit and provides something meaningful to contemplate as the week begins. I often hear from readers who let me know that a particular issue seems to have been assembled just for them. My best guess as to why they and many of you enjoy reading these quick splashes is that Ripples invites you to deepen your understanding of yourself, the people and events you encounter, and the world in general. We humans are eager to make sense of things. We long for meaning.

One of the best current guesses as to why we dream at night is that it is our mind's attempt to create meaning out of the random bits of information and emotions that are zooming around in our psyche as we slumber. We take all these facts and thoughts and feelings and ideas and memories and weave together a story. (It's one of the reasons that we can sometimes incorporate into our dream a noise or disturbance that doesn't completely wake us: we're so eager to create meaning that we will just add that into the story line we're dreaming about!) This doesn't just happen when we sleep, of course, because we are *always* trying to deepen our understanding of things.

Because people tend to seek and/or create meaning from a variety of sources (religion, philosophy, science, literature, etc.), I'll admit that at times I find it tricky to share a few ideas in a way that can be received by folks with a wide array of perspectives. Sometimes when I'm feeling feisty I'll admit to pushing the envelope; for the most part, however, I'm trying to gently nudge us all to be curious, thoughtful, mindful meaning-makers. Let's try to be a little more conscious this week of when and how we draw conclusions and make decisions about the people, events, and circumstances that cross our paths. Perhaps a bit more mindfulness will lead to a bit more useful meaning? Let's find out!

    Peace,
    Paul

RIPPLES NUMBER 998

Becoming You

PEBBLE

"Our job in this life is not to shape ourselves into some ideal we imagine we ought to be, but to find out who we already are and become it."

—STEVEN PRESSFIELD, SHARED BY JOSH S. IN LOS ANGELES

BOULDER

"There is no such thing as a perfect version of you. Every day you'll make choices that change who you're going to be. Who you're becoming is not finished. Which means you can be different, no matter who you've been up till now."

—BRIAN ANDREAS SHARED BY OUR FRIEND D,
WHO SAVORS THE SLOPES AND THE SEA

PONDER

So, how are you? And while I'm at it: Who are you? We often answer the first question with "fine" even when we aren't, and usually respond to the second with our name and maybe our occupation.

I've been lately pondering the longer, deeper answers to both of these questions, and encouraging workshop participants and keynote audiences to do the same. In many presentations, I invite people to form small groups and introduce themselves to each other in ways other than describing their work/education background. As I walk around the room, I hear some people talking about their families (the ones they were born into or the ones they've grown into), while others disclose places they've lived or visited. Other possible topics include hobbies, community engagement, or even favorite movies, books, or songs.

I also provide questions that make it easier to move beyond simple, trite answers about how work or life is going. Even posing this simple pair of questions can evoke (or elicit) longer, more meaningful conversations: What's working for you right now? What isn't? Pondering, sharing, and discussing these questions can help us better understand who we are and who we are becoming.

Of course our answers will continue to evolve. One of the exciting aspects of personal and professional growth is that today's answers have the power to reshape the responses you'll have tomorrow. Join us in the pondering, sharing, discussing, and becoming!

    Peace,
    Paul

RIPPLES NUMBER 1030

Thriving in the Mess

PEBBLE

"I always thought that the 'thriving' would come when everything was perfect, and what I learned is that it's actually down in the mess that things get good."

—JOANNA GAINES, SHARED BY LESLIE IN MADISON, WI

BOULDER

"I don't have to be perfect. All I have to do is show up and enjoy the messy, imperfect, and beautiful journey of my life. It's a trip more wonderful than I could have imagined."

—KERRY WASHINGTON, SHARED BY BRENDA IN DALLAS, TX

PONDER

Today's pebble and boulder are attributed to strong women who have faced adversity and figured out how to embrace life's inevitable difficulties as opportunities for growth. (I also happen to know that the women who *submitted* these quotes have endured their share of difficulty—and are still alive and kicking, too!)

It's fairly common to believe that our Best Life begins only when we get a grip on all the big stuff we're currently struggling with AND solve all the tiny and titanic problems that have bubbled up in our lives. It's a mythical yet tempting concoction of "the grass is always greener" and "the future will be better," and "Tomorrow Me will have everything together way more than Today Me does."

Here's the thing: while they might be nice to have, it turns out we don't absolutely NEED greener grass or a brighter future or a Better Me in order to thrive. We just need to embrace today's grass and today's opportunities and Today Me. Even the toughest days usually have some nuggets of goodness and joy to be savored, and it's more than possible to get stuff done even when our Best Me isn't available for appearances on a particular day. The bonus treat is that any time Today Me is able to eek out even a teensy bit of progress, it makes things easier and better for Tomorrow Me. (I know for certain that Today Me is deeply appreciative of so many things that several versions of Yesterday Me accomplished.)

So, join us (me and Joanna and Leslie and Kerry and Brenda) in thriving amidst whatever messiness exists in life right now. Invite Today You to cut Yesterday You some slack while tackling a few things to help Tomorrow You thrive even more. Work some, play some, and grow some. And go to bed early enough to rest up so we can do it all again with Tomorrow You. Are you in?

Peace,
Paul

RIPPLES NUMBER 822

The Power to Choose

PEBBLE

"Between stimulus and response there is a space. In that space is our power to choose our response. In our response lies our growth and our freedom."

—VIKTOR E. FRANKL, SHARED BY LAURETTA IN CINCINNATI, OH

BOULDER

"One's philosophy is not best expressed in words; it is expressed in the choices one makes; and the choices we make are ultimately our responsibility."

—ELEANOR ROOSEVELT, SHARED BY PETE IN SEDONA, AZ

PONDER

I look forward to watching the Oscars every year. I love watching movies, I crave the spectacle of the gala, and I'm curious to observe the host tackling the unique challenge of managing the tension and egos of the attendees in the theater while simultaneously entertaining the audience AND keeping the producers from pulling their hair out.

Well, last night at 7:58 p.m., my cable & internet service went out. I didn't know how long it would be out, but I guessed (correctly, it turns out) that I would miss at least the first part of the show which sets the mood and the tone. OHHHHHH, I was crushed. For about 25 seconds. I then remembered the Viktor Frankl quote on the opposite page. And I remembered that I didn't get to choose whether the Academy Awards were going to blip back to life. I didn't get to choose whether the cable company would treat this as the red alarm, DEFCON 1, lives-hanging-in-the-balance emergency that it initially seemed like to me.

The choice I DID have was how to respond. I took a deep breath, and remembered that my lights were still on (many of my neighbors had no power). I recognized that while my plans were halted, I was still comfortably warm in my cozy home and I had just about everything else I needed (food, clothes, shelter, friends, job, etc.). I took another deep breath, smiled, shared the bummer news with my FaceBuddies, and crawled into bed with my Kindle and my Grendel.

It wasn't the evening I had planned, but it wasn't bad at all. I woke up this morning and realized that my world wasn't ruined and I had more choices to make. My first thought was to go online and watch excerpts and find out who won. But then I realized that the issue of Ripples that was all queued up would need to wait until next week so I could share my adventure in choices. This is longer than usual because it is 6:52 a.m. and I didn't have time to edit if I was going to make my usual 7 a.m. sending. (Sorry if it's a few minutes late!). I'll quickly wrap this up and hope that you can be more aware of the choices YOU have about how to respond to the challenges you face today.

Peace,
Paul

RIPPLES NUMBER 901

Embracing Wholeness

PEBBLE

"We are not meant to be perfect, we are meant to be whole."

—JANE FONDA, SHARED BY BARBARA IN ROCHESTER, MI

BOULDER

"Wholeness does not mean perfection: it means embracing brokenness as an integral part of life. Knowing this gives me hope that human wholeness—mine, yours, ours—need not be a utopian dream if we can use devastation as a seedbed for new life."

—PARKER PALMER

"You are whole and also part of larger and larger circles of wholeness you may not even know about. You are never alone. And you already belong. You belong to humanity. You belong to life. You belong to this moment, this breath."

—JON KABAT-ZINN

PONDER

I've repeatedly encountered this magical word WHOLENESS lately, and it has caused me to ponder what it means to recognize and embrace our wholeness. The process of becoming whole seems to be about recognizing that we are already whole. Each of us is a unique collection of strengths and quirks and talents and opportunities for growth. We all contain in our souls both incredible light and considerable darkness; to deny the existence of either is to extend an illusion that shields us from our wholeness.

We can fulfill our grandest potential only when we are able to humbly and cheerfully acknowledge both our gifts and our shortcomings. Wholeness is also accepting the paradox that we are both completely independent from and yet inevitably dependent upon the people around us. We are at our best when we can stand on our own while relying on a tribe of friends, family, neighbors, and colleagues to lean on.

Our wholeness is even evident in our brokenness: those inevitable chapters in our life when we feel helpless, hopeless, and/or completely lost. Even then, there exists within us the capacity to take a deep breath (or three) and remember that the harder that life has been lately, the more impressive it is that we've made it to today. Embrace your whole, fabulous self this week. I feel certain it will improve your life, and it will probably impact the lives of those around you as well.

    Peace,
    Paul

RIPPLES NUMBER 925

Love's Shine

PEBBLE

"Love's shine is strongest against a backdrop of hate. What we care about, and how we express our care, is most deeply felt when all is not "as it should be." That's when love matters most and moves most."

—MELANIE GOBLE, WRITTEN AND SHARED BY MELANIE IN SAN LUIS OBISPO, CA

BOULDER

"To feel the love of people whom we love is a fire that feeds our life. But to feel affection that comes from those whom we do not know, from those unknown to us, who are watching over our sleep and solitude, over our dangers and our weaknesses: that is something still greater and more beautiful because it widens out the boundaries of our being and unites all living things."

—PABLO NERUDA, SHARED BY BRETT IN MADISON, WI

PONDER

Unleashing a LOVE-themed Ripples around Valentine's Day is one of our longest traditions, and it has always been important to me that we focus on the broadest concept of love that allows us to move beyond romance and celebrate the love that exists among friends, family, colleagues, neighbors and even beyond humans to include pets, nature, etc. We've also made an extra effort to encourage self-love as a powerful healing force directed within and toward your own precious spirit.

In these tumultuous times, I think it's crucial that we extend our idea of love even further. I'm ready to embrace a love so expansive that it encapsulates humanity and reminds us that we really are all connected to each other, and I hope you're ready for that as well. I truly believe that at least part of the solution for our current difficulties is to cultivate and strengthen the love we feel for each other, particularly toward those with whom we struggle to understand and agree.

I'm not necessarily talking about liking or understanding or accepting or agreeing or forgiving (although I do happen to think our society improves whenever we experiment a bit with these as well). Instead, I'm curious whether small doses of compassion, empathy, and patience, shared mindfully in the right direction at the right time, might help us all feel better, think more clearly, and identify opportunities for constructive conversations and connections. While it cannot and should not eliminate any important and necessary conflict we're experiencing in our world right now, I believe LOVE'S SHINE could help us illuminate a path forward, and might just end up saving us all.

    Peace,
    Paul

RIPPLES NUMBER 1035

Healing from Hurts

PEBBLE

"If you never heal from what hurt you, then you'll bleed on people who did not cut you."

—KAREN SALMANSOHN, SHARED BY TINA IN LANCASTER, PA

BOULDER

"Even when the wound is not your fault, healing from it is your responsibility."

—ADAPTED FROM UNKNOWN, SHARED BY CHRISTIE IN DEARBORN, MI

PONDER

At our best, we human beings are pretty nifty creatures; a powerful combination of tenderness and toughness. We have developed unique capabilities to cultivate joy (for celebrating good times) and to bolster reserves of tenacity and resilience (for enduring and recovering from inevitable difficulties that are part of a full life).

Illness, injury, and other challenges can knock us off center, depleting our energy and our effectiveness and even reducing our capacity for joy. With proper rest and recovery we eventually return to our former glory, perhaps with a few scars and hopefully with some experience and wisdom to help us in our future endeavors.

Here are some questions to ponder this week:

- What needs healing in your body, mind, and/or spirit right now?
- How might your effectiveness and/or enjoyment improve if you were to prioritize healing?
- How would others around you benefit from your healing?
- Could you work to resolve any internal blocks or external barriers that are keeping you from healing?
- Is healing worth it? What are you waiting for?
- If you've been feeling stuck, is it time to ask for help from friends or trained professionals?
- Would it help to forgive yourself and/or others for unhealed injuries? Can you?
- If you're in solid shape right now, is there anyone around you that could use your support on their healing journey?

I hope you find answers to the questions that can help you heal the most.

Peace,
Paul

RIPPLES NUMBER 881

Letting Go

PEBBLE

"Knowledge is learning something every day. Wisdom is letting go of something every day."

—ZEN PROVERB, SHARED BY TERRY IN OAK CREEK, WI

BOULDER

"Learning to let go should be learned before learning to get. Life should be touched, not strangled. You've got to relax, let it happen at times, and at others move forward with it."

—RAY BRADBURY

PONDER

We are made to grieve. Whether you think we humans were created from High Above, or that we evolved from the deepest ocean depths, or something in between or even altogether different, it seems clear that included in our operating system is the capacity to endure loss.

We sometimes tell children stories about where their beloved pets or favorite toys have gone, but fairly early on we are able grasp the idea that animals and toys eventually go away. And people, too. We are often sad for a while, and usually experience some frustration and other emotions. Eventually, though, we come to terms with letting go. And then we figure out how to move forward.

The same is true of our thoughts. As we grow through life, the information we pick up and the ways we look at the world sometimes become outdated. Even "facts" like how many planets there are in our solar system can evolve as our understandings and perspectives shift. Some people are more amenable to change and therefore more adaptable; it's also true that some things are easier to let go of than others. But one thing is as true for great losses as it is for our grudges and our gadgets: the ability to survive and thrive as we meander through this topsy-turvy life depends significantly upon our ability to let go.

You or someone you care about may be in the process of saying goodbye to a person or a situation or a way of looking at the world. While we can't rush ourselves or our loved ones through the process, there is great benefit to be found in identifying our thoughts and feelings, letting ourselves THINK and FEEL deeply, and to be consciously curious about when and how to let go.

    Peace,
    Paul

RIPPLES NUMBER 882

The Journey of Un-Becoming

PEBBLE

"Maybe the journey isn't so much about becoming anything. Maybe it's about un-becoming everything that isn't really you, so you can be who you were meant to be in the first place."

—UNKNOWN (FOUND VIA @PURPOSEFAIRY),
SHARED BY PAT IN BRUEGGERTON, CLIFTONIA

BOULDER

"Stop trying to heal yourself, fix yourself, even awaken yourself. Let go of letting go. Stop trying to fast-forward the movie of your life, chasing futures that never seem to arrive. Instead, bow deeply to yourself as you actually are. Your pain, your sorrow, your doubts, your deepest longings, your fearful thoughts are not mistakes, and they aren't asking to be healed. They are asking to be held. Here, now, lightly, in the loving arms of present awareness."

—JEFF FOSTER SHARED BY STEPHANY NEAR CHEROKEE MARSH, WI

PONDER

We are, each of us, on a journey. Many people believe that their particular path was either divinely designed just FOR them, or on some level chosen BY them for the unique combination of lessons and opportunities it offers. You could say it is the Trip of a Lifetime, and whether our itineraries were created by the Great Travel Agency Above, self-selected, or simply randomly assigned, it's most assuredly up to US to make the most of the adventure.

Michelangelo described his process of sculpting as seeing a statue in an ordinary block of marble and then chipping away the excess material until the figure was revealed. Perhaps this week's quotes are an invitation to shift away from viewing life as a series of "we must make something of ourselves" obligations and instead imagining a sampling of "let's reveal our natural splendor" opportunities.

I propose we purposefully pause the momentum of go, go, go, and grow, grow, grow this week; let's catch our breath and unpack some of the baggage we've been lugging around. We can leave behind any past hurts, broken promises, unrealistic expectations, and expired dreams that have slowed us down which will allow us to travel lighter and freer and perhaps have a little extra room for new trinkets and possibilities along the way.

Enjoy the next leg of your trip, and send me a postcard along the way!

Peace,
Paul

RIPPLES NUMBER 978

Being Tender

PEBBLE

"Gentle. Kind. Friendly."

—GRAMMA JANICE SHARED BY KYLEE IN RACINE, WI,
(who has long valued this simple-yet-sage advice that her mother-in-law shared with the students she taught as well as her own children and grandchildren whenever she witnessed them not getting along.)

BOULDER

"Being tender and open is beautiful. Don't let someone steal your tenderness. Don't allow the coldness and fear of others to tarnish your perfectly vulnerable beating heart. Nothing is more powerful than allowing yourself to truly be affected by things. Whether it's a song, a stranger, a mountain, a raindrop, a tea kettle, an article, a sentence, a footstep, feel it all: look around you. All of this is for you. Take it and have gratitude. Give it and feel love."

—ZOOEY DESCHANEL

PONDER

There is quite a bit of meanness out there these days. I've noticed it in the news, on social media, on the road while traveling, and throughout the world. There's niceness too, of course. But I'm convinced that over the last few years we have depleted our collective reserves of trust, respect, and positive regard toward our fellow humans; it's left us with raw nerves and reduced compassion.

When we encounter a grumpity-grump or a meanie-beanie, our first instinct can be to jump into defensive mode. I've too often found myself barking right back at someone before I fully realize what is actually going on. This frequently happens when we're "emotionally hijacked," a term that describes what happens inside our bodies and minds when we activate our instinctual fight-or-flight reflex. This process has noble intentions to preserve and protect, but too often leads us to say and/or do things that we later end up regretting or rationalizing.

With all that is going on in our world, there are plenty of legitimate reasons to be frustrated. While it's important to our individual and collective well-being that we express our emotions, it's equally important that we make time to pause so we can avoid reacting rashly and instead respond mindfully. That pause is not always easy, but it's almost always worth it since it helps to ensure we're bringing our best self to the situation. You know, the self that knows the importance of being tender and also remembers the value of "Gentle. Kind. Friendly."

Peace,
Paul

RIPPLES NUMBER 717

Mini-Puzzles

PEBBLE

"If you find a path with no obstacles, it probably doesn't lead anywhere."

—FRANK A. CLARK, SHARED BY SUSAN IN WOODLAND, CA

BOULDER

"It's life's complexities that make it fun; mini-puzzles all over the place just waiting to be skillfully solved!"

—WRITTEN AND SHARED BY HOLLY FROM SOUTH JERSEY

PONDER

Life ain't always easy. Depending upon what your life is currently like, your reaction to this statement could range anywhere from a slight nod and shrug all the way up to a sarcastic, "Duh!" or maybe even all the way to screaming, "TELL ME SOMETHING I DON'T KNOW, AND THEN TELL ME HOW TO FIX MY CRAPPY LIFE!" The bad news is that I don't likely have the answers to fix all the challenges you're facing right now.

The good news is that there are more answers within you than you might realize, and one of the most useful ways to transform obstacles into opportunities is to change how you view them. The trick is to tweak your attitude just a bit; shift your perspective enough to see your current difficulties as mini-puzzles that, once solved, will help you acquire new skills. The bigger the puzzle, the more difficult this can be AND the more lessons you can learn from it.

Of course, shifting your attitude alone won't solve the puzzles. It will, however, unlock significant internal resources to help you get started.

Peace,
Paul

RIPPLES NUMBER 1018

Finding & Unfurling Joy

PEBBLE

"Joy comes to us in ordinary moments. We risk missing out on joy when we get too busy chasing down the extraordinary."

—BRENÉ BROWN, SHARED BY RACHEL IN ROCHESTER, MI

BOULDER

"Happiness is a form of power: it's carbonated consciousness that wants to spill out and be articulated. So if we downplay our joy we confuse our nervous system. Our brain is trying to fire happy neurons but our cool or too quiet behavior is short dousing the positive chemicals. Repeated happiness-muffling numbs our senses. And if you keep your joy under the surface too long, it might stay there. If you're happy and you know it ... show it."

—DANIELLE LAPORTE, SHARED BY ONE OF OUR ORIGINAL RIPPLERS

PONDER

There are two aspects of joy I've been pondering lately: its availability, and its source. I love the big delightful versions of joy that show up around the holidays and other special occasions: monumental moments of spectacular awe that can light up a room and light up our lives. Since those big joys can be relatively few and far between, it's good to keep in mind that joy can also be found in the ordinary days that make up most of our existence. Small delights like a string of traffic lights turning green, an unexpected discount on one of our favorite grocery items, or finding a crumpled up $5 bill while doing laundry (OK, so that just happened to me a few days ago and it was joyous, indeed!) have the power to bring joy when we notice them.

The other thing I like about joy is that I don't have to wait for it to show up in order for me to experience it. I've come to rely on the premise that there are tiny pockets of joy stored in my consciousness waiting to be noticed and unleashed. At times they get activated by an external trigger: a friend will call or a song will pop up on Pandora and Joy starts dancing. But it's also been my experience that I can consciously elicit joy when the need arises. Maybe that means picking up the phone instead of waiting for it to ring, pressing play on some of the playlists I've purposely curated as joyful, or playing a game of "set the timer for 20 minutes to earn 20 minutes of game time."

Assembling this issue of Ripples has me eager to experiment with finding and unfurling joy ... perhaps you'll join me in this experiment?

    Peace,
    Paul

RIPPLES NUMBER 832

Allowing Others In

PEBBLE

"Spiritual growth is characterized by the capacity to allow others into your heart."

—TIJN TOUBER, SHARED BY TERRY IN OAK CREEK, WI

BOULDER

"A blessed thing it is for any man or woman to have a friend, one human soul whom we can trust utterly, who knows the best and worst of us, and who loves us in spite of all our faults."

—CHARLES KINGSLEY, SHARED BY NICK IN INDIANA

PONDER

It isn't always easy to let someone into your heart to develop an authentic connection with them. Sometimes it's our personality that prefers to keep emotions at bay and connections at arm's length; other times it's the norms we picked up from our families, communities, and/or cultures that dictates how close we get to those around us. It's also true that past hurts sometimes create protective coatings to safeguard us. And while they have incredibly noble aspirations of preventing us from being hurt, they also unfortunately keep out empathy and compassion that is being extended by those with noble intentions and worthy goals. Those people want to love us, but we are sometimes too afraid to let them in.

The first step to allowing others into the sacred and softer places in our heart is to notice both the benefits and costs of keeping people at a distance, and seeing if there aren't some small risks we could take to let someone in just a bit. Might you be willing to experiment this week: try sharing a bit of personal information with a colleague you've spoken with several times, or opening up to a neighbor or acquaintance that you've known superficially for years? I'm in if you are!

Peace,
Paul

P.S. I was inspired to assemble this week's Ripples by recent encounters with a few remarkable people who are taking courageous steps to emerge from their protective casings and seek the healing embrace of vulnerability and connectedness. I extend my kudos to them, and an invitation to the rest of us to allow others in this week.

"The beautiful spring came, and when nature resumes her loveliness, the human soul is apt to revive also."

—HARRIET ANN JACOBS

spring

RIPPLES NUMBER 1034

Spring Blossoms

PEBBLE

"Spring can blossom in my heart even before it blossoms in the soil."

—JULIE INGRAM, WRITTEN AND SHARED BY JULIE IN CHRISTIANSBURG, VA

BOULDER

"If we had no winter, the spring would not be so pleasant; if we did not sometimes taste of adversity, prosperity would not be so welcome."

—ANNE BRADSTREET, SHARED BY THOMAS IN FT. MYERS, FL

PONDER

While we are just a few days away from the official start of spring, there may be things keeping you from anticipating a sense of renewal that we tend to associate with its arrival. The weather, a hectic schedule, or just some big "stuff" on your plate right now could dampen your mood and prevent you from embracing an "it's time to sprout" mindset.

Even if the temperature or your to-do list isn't cooperating, perhaps you could consider experimenting with some internal spring cleaning:

- Declutter thoughts and feelings. Jot down a list of things that have been festering lately and decide which can be easily tossed out and which ones need tending.
- Plant some new habits. Identify a couple of activities that would increase effectiveness and/or enjoyment in work or life and experiment with cultivating routines that allow them to happen.
- Clean up past hurts. If there are psychic wounds that need tending to, it may be time to extend an olive branch and ask for forgiveness or make time to connect with a counselor (or trusted friend) to process unfinished work.
- Stretch. Just as it's important to warm up muscles before we start exercising, we can also prepare for an upcoming growth spurt by stretching beyond our comfort zone. Tackling a challenging project, taking up a new hobby, or even watching a movie from a "not your usual genre" can help as we grow into the next version of ourselves.

Keep in mind that each day only has a minute or two of added daylight this time of year, and yet those small shifts will soon add up to a few extra hours of daylight each and every day. Small, daily efforts now can lead to sunnier, more enjoyable days quite soon!

Peace,
Paul

RIPPLES NUMBER 927

Celebrating Struggle

PEBBLE

"The tests of life are to make you, not break you."

—NORMAN VINCENT PEALE, SHARED BY TOM IN JEFFERSON, WI

BOULDER

"It is okay to be at a place of struggle. Struggle is just another word for growth. Even the most evolved beings find themselves in a place of struggle now and then. In fact, struggle is a sure sign to them that they are expanding; it is their indication of real and important progress. The only one who doesn't struggle is the one who doesn't grow. So if you are struggling right now, see it as a terrific sign—celebrate your struggle."

—NEALE DONALD WALSCH, SHARED BY CODY IN LAKEWOOD, WA

PONDER

I'm sorry if you're struggling right now, but I'm also kind of excited for you. As tough as things are at this particular moment, I'm guessing that if you can summon the strength and courage to continue on a bit longer, all kinds of rewards are eagerly waiting for you at the finish line (or at the next break station if your current struggle is more of a marathon!).

If you've been on overdrive for too long, you may need to rest up and perhaps even ask for some help. And for goodness' sake, don't be embarrassed or ashamed to ask for help. We sometimes forget that seeking assistance is a sign of character strength and *not* an indication of weakness or meekness.

Lastly, remember just how strong you are! Past struggles often temporarily tucker us out for a short time but ultimately leave us tougher and wiser. Keeping this in mind makes it easier to identify reasons to celebrate the struggles we're facing today.

Peace,
Paul

P.S. If this finds you in a good place right now, and you're not significantly struggling, I have TWO favors to ask: First, spend a little time pondering struggles you've endured in the past few years and congratulate yourself on moving through them. Secondly, perhaps you can keep an eye out for someone in your life who IS struggling mightily at this time and go out of your way to give them a hand. Even a simple note to let them know that you're aware of the difficulty they are facing can help someone feel less alone.

RIPPLES NUMBER 107

Ripples of Kindness

PEBBLE

"No act of kindness, no matter how small, is ever wasted."

—AESOP, SHARED BY STEPHANIE

BOULDER

"The teacher asked her pupils to tell the meaning of loving-kindness. A little boy jumped up and said, 'Well, if I was hungry and someone gave me a piece of bread that would be kindness; but if they put jelly on it that would be loving-kindness!'"

—ORIGINAL SOURCE UNKNOWN, SHARED BY LARISSA M.

PONDER

Recently, I had the opportunity to hang out with some emerging leaders at Nebraska Wesleyan University, and we discussed the importance of smiles. For most of us, the natural look on our face is perceived by others as serious, troubling, or even sad. This may be true for you if people frequently ask, "Is everything okay?" or "Are you upset?" when they pass you in the hallway.

In my many airport adventures, I am astonished at how serious and troubled everyone looks. As I flew home to Wisconsin, I was determined to smile as much as possible on my layover journey between concourses (which are always planned by airlines to maximize the opportunity for exercise!). Most people didn't even make eye contact, and when they did it was just a brief glance and then a return to their own hurried journey. At one point, however, as I traveled along a moving sidewalk with my bags resting on the platform, my eyes connected with a woman who was moving in the opposite direction. As I smiled and nodded at her, the most amazing thing happened: she smiled back! Not a quick forced grimace, nor was it a big, creepy smile that would surely have frightened me. Instead, a wide, genuine grin spread across her face and for a brief instant it was as though two old friends had reconnected. In a flash the moment had passed, but for the rest of the trip I felt all warm inside. I felt important, I felt acknowledged, I felt connected.

So, do me a favor and change the world this week by putting jelly on your face: smile!

Peace,
Paul

Knowing Yourself

PEBBLE

"Drop the idea of becoming someone, because you are already a masterpiece. You cannot be improved. You have only to come to it, to know it, to realize it."

—OSHO, SHARED BY PETE IN OURAY, CO

BOULDER

"You've got to know yourself. You've got to know what ignites your magic, what fires your soul into performing majestic acts of love. You've got to know yourself so much that not even a hundred voices will drown yours. You've got to own yourself: this journey is all yours. All yours. No one can do it and you decide whenever you are ready to embark on it. Unlearn, learn, master yourself and love yourself or else they will define you and that's a poisonous kind of life. That's death."

—IJEOMA UMEBINYUO, SHARED BY SIMONE IN RENO, NV

PONDER

I talk. A lot. When I'm on the road, I talk to audiences; when I'm home I talk to my friends and neighbors. If you've ever spotted me on my morning walks or as I scoot through the airport on my travels, you know that I even talk to myself.

Talking, along with listening, are two important ways that I connect with the world. It allows me to build and deepen connections with others. It also allows me to deepen the connection I have with my inner self.

I think I've been talking to myself since forever, but it took an interesting turn while in counseling and I'd say something to my therapist like, "I don't know why I sometimes do that." And she'd say, "Why don't you ask yourself?" I was surprised at how often I could pose a question internally then wait just a moment before a response surfaced. I was also surprised at how often the answer surprised me. I'd be reminded of something I hadn't thought about in ages, or an entirely new thought would emerge.

I'd like to invite you to have some inner conversations this week; spend some time posing questions that you might ask a friend or even someone you're just getting to know: "How are you? What's working in your life right now? What isn't? What can I do to help you grow?"

It may feel a little awkward at first, and you might not receive (or recognize) a response right away. With a little practice, though, it might help you get to know yourself a little better. I believe it's worth a try, because I believe you're worth a try.

Peace,
Paul

RIPPLES NUMBER 1037

Comparison Hangover

PEBBLE

"You can only compare your current self to your former self. You'll get a comparison hangover if you constantly measure your worth against someone else."

—DAX SHEPHERD, SHARED BY NORA IN SHALIMAR, FL

BOULDER

"Your opponent, in the end, is never really the player on the other side of the net, or the swimmer in the next lane, or the team on the other side of the field, or even the bar you must high-jump. Your opponent is yourself, your negative internal voices, your level of determination."

—GRACE LICHTENSTEIN

PONDER

Comparing ourselves to others is an easy habit to fall into even though it tends to alternatively feed our insecurities (when we compare ourselves to those who seem to be doing it all effortlessly and excellently) and our ego (when we observe those who have stumbled and we can temporarily feel better about ourselves with a snarky, "Well, at least I'm not in THAT situation.").

It's an inevitable part of being human and yet it's frequently more destructive than it is developmental. It can create unrealistic expectations that might temporarily give us something to aspire to, but then eventually damage our confidence and diminish our hope when we fall far short. Other times it can cause us to reach unhelpful and inaccurate conclusions about our value and our potential when we subtly transition from, "I guess I wasn't as ____ as I thought I was," to "I guess I'm just not that ____."

If you've been doing lots of comparing yourself to others, see if you can notice it without judging yourself too harshly. Instead of trying to quickly eliminate the comparison, perhaps let it illuminate: get curious about why you're comparing yourself and whether there is a more helpful way to achieve the same goal.

Striving for excellence helps maximize your potential. Trying to be like someone else is a recipe for disaster. You can't be just like them because that job is already taken, and in the meantime, you'll miss out on becoming the best possible version of yourself.

Peace,
Paul

RIPPLES NUMBER 666

Quirky You

PEBBLE

"Embrace your uniqueness. Time is much too short to be living someone else's life."

—SOURCE UNKNOWN

BOULDER

"You know those things about yourself that you're self-conscious of? Those quirks that you're trying to hide? Those are not your weaknesses, those are your strengths."

—TERRY BORDER, SHARED BY SAMANTHA IN NEW HAMPSHIRE

PONDER

You're weird. Yeah, you kinda are. But here's the deal: your quirks don't show you're flawed, they prove you are fabulous. So stop trying to hide in the shadows; the world really needs you to shine.

It might feel a little uncomfortable at first, but you'll soon notice that it will help you bring your full and best self to every day. And bonus: you'll be inviting those around you to do the same. When that happens, everyone wins!

    Peace,
    Paul

RIPPLES NUMBER 966

The Tensions and the Doldrums

PEBBLE

"We grow and learn the most during the tension we experience in life."

—ASHLEY LORAH WRITTEN AND SHARED BY ASHLEY IN COLUMBUS, OH
(who has been facing challenges by looking ahead to get excited about the growth that will come from them rather than dwelling on the difficulties themselves)

BOULDER

"It has been liberating to allow myself to feel and experience life so intensely, to go through the doldrums, and then to come out of them having learned something about myself."

—J. HARDIN *(adapted)* SHARED BY LESLIE IN MADISON, WI

PONDER

I'm not gonna lie: I've been dealing with some rather unpleasant STUFF lately, including challenges related to my physical health and a few wrinkles with my mental health. Add in the steady stream of really heavy news stories over the past several months ... well, it's a recipe for feeling less than my best self. (Understatement, you have a call on line one.)

The good news is that all of this STUFF didn't prevent me from having some truly lovely moments over the holidays, and I continue to have a really strong support base that I've been able to consistently depend on over the last several weeks. The bad news is that it's gonna take some time and effort to get myself back to my usual self and my usual life, and the progress is gonna be more gradual than I would prefer. (Control issues, you have a call on line two.)

As I sat down to pull together this issue of Ripples, I confessed to my boyfriend that I wasn't feeling very Ripply and for the first time in a really long time I didn't quite know how to summon the right energy and mindset to pull together something uplifting to zoom out on Monday morning. His response was significant and powerful: "Paul, what if you just shared exactly what you are thinking? Lots of other people might be feeling less than stellar either because of all the carbs they ate, or coming down from the high of being around loved ones, or just the letdown of the holiday being over." I immediately recalled the "doldrums" quote Leslie had shared with me a while back and knew it would make a good base on which to build this issue. It took only another moment to match it with the simple yet powerful words that Ashley shared quite recently, which reminded me of a consistent truth in my life: I've always learned more during the tough chapters of my life than the easy-breezy ones.

Now I'm feeling better about not feeling better than I do, so I can exhale and get back to letting myself feel exactly the way I do. And the irony is that I can already sense the tensions lifting and the doldrums dissipating.

Peace,
Paul

RIPPLES NUMBER 1036

Your Reason, Your Dance

PEBBLE

"One reason you're on this planet is to discover all the reasons you're on this planet. Go find your reasons!"

—CORY MOEN, WRITTEN AND SHARED BY CORY IN KEARNEY, NE

BOULDER

"There is a dance only you can do, that exists only in you, here and now, always changing, always true. Are you willing to listen with fascination? If you are, it will deliver you unto the self you have always dreamed you could be. This is a promise."

—GABRIELLE ROTH, SHARED BY PETE IN SEDONA, AZ

PONDER

I had an engaging exchange with Cory about his emerging life philosophy that we feature as today's pebble. I particularly liked his reminder that finding meaning and purpose in life is an ongoing process and not a "once you find it then you're done" kind of thing.

I also like the perspective that there isn't just One Thing we're here to do in this lifetime. We might find different reasons for different areas of our lives (work, home, community, etc.), and we also might have directions that evolve over time. One period in our lives might be really focused on one particular goal, and then we get to another chapter and find that it's time to move in a different direction and focus on something entirely different.

What I love most about his philosophy is that finding purpose isn't a passive process where you just sit and wait around for it to show up. Meaning is more likely to make itself known if we're out and about in the world, taking chances and trying different things.

If you're in a groove right now with a solid sense of direction, take some time this week to celebrate! If you're struggling or just feeling a little lost at the moment, take heart: finding your dance is sometimes difficult, and most of us experience at least occasional periods of feeling lost and unable to hear any music at all.

It might be helpful to keep your eyes open for opportunities to try new things that the universe plants in your path. Tackling a new project, or sampling a new hobby or community-service effort might help you find a new rhythm.

Alternatively, it could be useful to just sit in the not knowing and notice what it's like to not have a solid direction at the moment. You might learn a little something about yourself, and that might lead to an insight that leads you in a new direction.

Peace,
Paul

RIPPLES NUMBER 773

Throwing Back

PEBBLE

"I've learned that you shouldn't go through life with a catcher's mitt on both hands. You need to be able to throw something back."

—MAYA ANGELOU, SHARED BY COURTNEY IN SAN LUIS OBISPO, CA

BOULDER

"Since you cannot do good to all, you are to pay special attention to those who, by the accidents of time, or place, or circumstances, are brought into closer connection with you."

—AUGUSTINE OF HIPPO, SHARED BY RYAN IN LA CROSSE, WI

PONDER

I know you know this, but let's review: life can be awesome, and life can be awful. No matter how many years you've been on this planet, chances are you've had lots of good days and more than a few bad days. And while no one else has experienced your unique combination of awesome and awful, it's essential to remember that every single person on this planet has their own mix of good and bad. This is true for each soul you encounter: your closest family, friends, neighbors, classmates, and colleagues as well as the folks you encounter occasionally and even the complete strangers that you'll cross paths with only once.

I believe the single most powerful thing you can do to improve the world is to consistently keep your eyes and ears open for small opportunities to help the people you encounter in your daily life. A warm smile, a quick favor, even a dollop of extra patience with someone who is "in your way" can be invaluable to someone who is struggling. Your calm presence in someone's chaotic life can be a godsend, and here is the bonus: It doesn't just help them, IT HELPS YOU, TOO! I know you've experienced that feeling of joy that arises when you're able to lend a hand, and I'm guessing you've recognized opportunities to pay it forward because others have been there for you in the past.

I'm not here on this planet to TEACH you about the value of creating ripples. I'm just here to remind you that your help is far more precious and valuable than you often realize. Do yourself and others a favor and throw something back today.

Peace,
Paul

RIPPLES NUMBER 948

Common Enchantment

PEBBLE

"We wait, starving for moments of high magic to inspire us, but life is full of common enchantment waiting for our alchemist's eyes to notice."

—JACOB NORDBY, SHARED BY VANESSA IN DES MOINES, IA

BOULDER

"In the best of times our days are numbered anyway, and so it would be a crime against nature for any generation to take the world's crisis so solemnly that it put off enjoying those things for which we were designed in the first place. The opportunity to do good work, to fall in love, to enjoy friends, to hit a ball, and to bounce a baby."

—ALISTAIR COOKE SHARED BY SHARON IN MADISON, WI

PONDER

The two quotes on the opposite page matched themselves up nicely, and then it was time to decide what I wanted to say about the idea of COMMON ENCHANTMENT. As I read over the quotes a few times and then stared off into space, I noticed a really colorful outfit someone walking through the airport was wearing. "How enchanting," I thought, and instantly realized that I needed to pause from pondering the IDEA of "common enchantment," and simply let myself BE enchanted by the delicious commonness that was all around me.

I began noticing people and sounds and decorations. I observed families getting excited about vacations, business colleagues huddling around laptops, and solo travelers immersed in books. I noticed sunbeams hitting a variety of surfaces, shadows creating patterns and depth, and so many more shades and hues than I usually notice. And not only was I aware of the beauty around me, the airport *sounded* enchanting as well: a cacophony of voices and music amidst all sorts of hustle and bustle.

I was so enchanted that I hadn't noticed boarding was nearly complete, and some fella named, "Wesselmann" was being paged to get on the plane. Whoops! I scooted my way over to the gate, down the jetway, and into my seat. The enchantment continued on board: the passengers seemed more interesting, the flight crew seemed friendlier, and the plane itself more intricate and wondrous than any of the hundreds of planes I've boarded over the years. An experience I've had so many times was transformed into an exquisite adventure with just the slightest of adjustments.

Now it is YOUR turn: close your eyes, take a few deep breaths, and when you open your eyes again, observe the COMMON ENCHANTMENT around you.

Peace,
Paul

RIPPLES NUMBER 806

Trust Your Power

PEBBLE

"The most common way people give up their power is by thinking they don't have any."

—ALICE WALKER, SHARED BY SARA IN ALEXANDRIA, VA

BOULDER

"A bird sitting on a tree is never afraid of the branch breaking, because her trust is not in the branch but in her own wings. Always believe in yourself."

—UNKNOWN, SHARED BY TAYLOR IN MINNEAPOLIS, MN

PONDER

Many people think about POWER in terms of influencing or controlling other people, and forget that it's mostly just about getting stuff done. And while there are real external obstacles that can sometimes keep us from doing what we want, there are plenty of situations where we inadvertently diminish our personal potential simply by ignoring or avoiding the power we have to make decisions and act in ways that lift us up.

If you've been frustrated recently by situations where you felt held back or denied, perhaps you can move forward this week by focusing instead on a choice that you DO have, an action you CAN take that will help you enhance your effectiveness and/or enjoyment. TRUSTING YOUR POWER is really about your confidence that you can get stuff done despite inevitable obstacles and setbacks.

You go, friend. YOU GO!

Peace,
Paul

RIPPLES NUMBER 908

Let Yourself In

PEBBLE

"The universe buries strange jewels deep within us all, and then stands back to see if we can find them."

—ELIZABETH GILBERT, SHARED BY HOLLY IN PHOENIX, AZ

BOULDER

"The core of yourself is never lost. Let go of all the pretending and becoming you've done just to belong. Curl up with your rawness and come home. You don't have to find yourself; you just have to let yourself in."

—D. ANTOINETTE FOY, SHARED BY LESLIE IN MADISON, WI

PONDER

The process of identifying quote pairs to make a good Pebble/Boulder combo is a little like playing a game of Concentration/Memory where you spread out a deck of cards face down and turn over two cards at a time with the goal of finding matches. I think these are both aces, although I confess I've been worrying they might not work well together since one of them implies an inner search while the other suggests we need to stop searching.

After placing them side by side for a few weeks, I gradually came to experience them as complementary clues for the Inner Exploration so many of us seem to be on lately. The pebble suggests we have gifts buried within; the boulder gently reminds us that we are not only the seekers of treasure, we are the gatekeepers as well. If your search for self has been spinning its wheels lately, what if you set aside the treasure map and acknowledge what you already know about yourself? Consider the gifts you've acquired, the talents you've cultivated, the achievements you've gained, and even the difficulties you've conquered that created opportunities to grow stronger and wiser.

Let yourself know all of this; let yourself delight in it; let yourself in!

    Peace,
    Paul

RIPPLES NUMBER 949

Slight Adjustments

PEBBLE

"We take almost all of the decisive steps in our lives as a result of slight inner adjustments of which we are barely conscious."

—W.G. SEBALD, ANOTHER GREAT FIND BY LESLIE IN MADISON, WI
(who has been scrounging up fabulous Pebbles and Boulders since our first year of Rippling ... way back in 1999!)

BOULDER

"Your life is like Tetris. Stop playing it like chess. It's choosing, on a fundamental level. It's taking these random experiences as they slowly fall down the screen of life and rotating them 360°; moving them two rows left and three to the right; examining them from new vantage points so as to make them fit into the grander mosaic of our lives. Tetris, not chess. If you think you're in checkmate, you can choose to flip the table and play something else."

—JEREMY MATHURIN, 2016 HAMILTON COLLEGE STUDENT COMMENCEMENT SPEAKER SHARED BY DAVE, SILVER SPRING, MD

PONDER

It can be tempting to daydream about the BIG shifts that we think would improve our lives: if only we could snag that dream job/house/relationship or radically improve the country/world/universe. Whenever I find myself lost in those daydreams, I try to remind myself that while the big changes sound exciting and life altering, it's the myriad small decisions we make each day that have a more significant impact on our lives.

Studying for the midterms and showing up for the final exam are essential, of course, but your daily decisions about whether to go to class and how many minutes you'll study have a far bigger impact on your academic success. It's important to go to the dentist a few times a year, but the bigger impact on your dental health are the daily decisions you make about whether to brush and floss. And while relationships can be deepened or destroyed by single events, most of our cherished connections are made by lots of small deposits: texts and chats and lunches and walks and such.

Let's make this week be about recognizing and seizing the small, everyday choices we have available to us, and explore how these SLIGHT ADJUSTMENTS might expand our options and improve our outlook.

    Peace,
    Paul

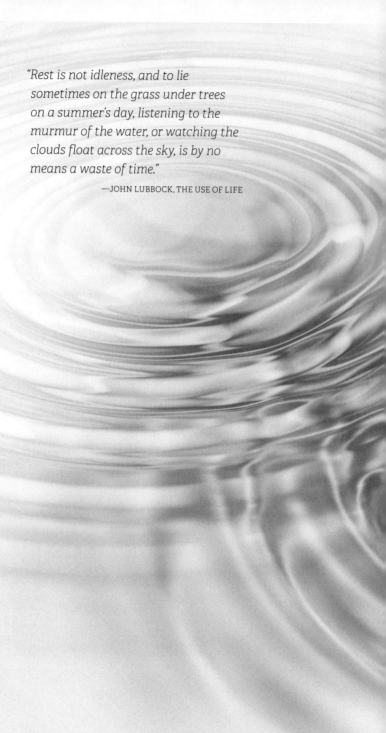

"Rest is not idleness, and to lie sometimes on the grass under trees on a summer's day, listening to the murmur of the water, or watching the clouds float across the sky, is by no means a waste of time."

—JOHN LUBBOCK, THE USE OF LIFE

summer

RIPPLES NUMBER 506

Rut Departure

PEBBLE

"You are closer to glory leaping an abyss than upholstering a rut."

—JAMES BROUGHTON, SHARED BY SARAH N., MADISON WI

BOULDER

"The truth is that our finest moments are most likely to occur when we are feeling deeply uncomfortable, unhappy, or unfulfilled. For it is only in such moments, propelled by our discomfort, that we are likely to step out of our ruts and start searching for different ways or truer answers."

—M. SCOTT PECK, SHARED BY PAT S., APPLETON, WI

PONDER

Ladies and gentleman, thank you for joining us on this flight to New Possibilities. We have been cleared for takeoff from the rut you have been in, so we need you to buckle your seat belt, allow your arms and legs to wave and jump enthusiastically, and note the emergency exits do not exist on this aircraft because you won't need them!

You are scheduled to arrive at a new destination with renewed passion and more energy than when you left your rut because you are excited and a little scared. This is the way it shall be. Enjoy your journey!

    Peace,
    Paul

RIPPLES NUMBER 883

Little Choices

PEBBLE

"The little choices of daily life determine our destiny."

—MARY DIXON THAYER, SHARED BY AL IN MARINETTE, WI

BOULDER

"Some people say, 'What is the sense of our small effort?' They cannot see that we must lay one brick at a time, take one step at a time. A pebble cast into a pond causes ripples that spread in all directions. Each one of our thoughts, words and deeds is like that. No one has a right to sit down and feel hopeless. There is too much work to do."

—DOROTHY DAY, SHARED BY LORA IN KENNEBUNK, ME

PONDER

It's tempting to revel in the grand gestures and big moments in our work and in our lives. I admit that sometimes standing on a huge stage in front of a massive audience can cause a surge of energy, and I've been known to feel extra proud of those social media posts that received out-sized responses. On my best days, however, I measure the success of my efforts in the smaller, quieter moments: providing encouraging words to someone who is facing big changes in their life, or learning that an unexpected tangent during a talk generated ongoing and useful insights. And while I'm genuinely excited that this message you're reading right now zooms out to lots and lots of people every Monday, there is a calm and humble joy that settles over me when I hear about a specific issue that helped a single person refresh their outlook or persist through difficulty.

It makes sense to me that we celebrate the marquee events like graduations and retirements and promotions that signal an increase in responsibility and/or opportunity. If you're getting ready to celebrate one of them: CONGRATS! Just remember to keep in mind that in between the massive milestones and big parties, there are countless ordinary opportunities for gradual progress that will help you and those around you maximize the potential of your day and your life.

Enjoy the big moments, enjoy the little choices, and enjoy today.

Peace,
Paul

P.S. Oh the irony! As I assemble this issue of Ripples about focusing on small moments over big events, I realize this will zoom in your direction on April 25th, the 19th anniversary of my first day of full-time self-employment as a leadership trainer and keynote speaker. Way back in 1997, I had no idea of the possibilities that existed for me, and these weekly splashes of inspiration hadn't even been conceived. I didn't know I was going to have this much fun in my work, and I never imagined having this many people along for the ride. I'll stick to this week's theme by thanking you for each Monday that you choose to open your heart and mind to Ripples, and each time you choose to extend the Ripples by passing them along to others. Namaste.

RIPPLES NUMBER 819

Museum of Beautiful Stuff

PEBBLE

"Think of the world you carry within you."

—RAINER MARIA RILKE, SHARED BY AMY IN TACOMA, WA

BOULDER

"We never sit anything out. We are cups, constantly and quietly being filled. The trick is knowing how to tip ourselves over and let the beautiful stuff out."

—RAY BRADBURY, SHARED BY ABBY IN CINCINNATI, OH

PONDER

You, my friend, are a living, breathing, moving museum: a constantly evolving exhibit of all the ideas and experiences you encounter. Every person you engage with and every adventure you undertake creates artwork and artifacts that are all contained within your spirit. You have choices to make about when and what to put on display; please be careful not to keep too many of them hidden. Your exhibition will remind others that beauty and discovery and awe still exist in this world, and you may encourage them to reveal their own hidden gems.

Don't forget to set the price of admission high enough to establish your worth, and yet low enough to welcome in the right folks.

    Peace,
    Paul

Refracting Peace

PEBBLE

"It isn't enough to talk about peace. One must believe in it. And it isn't enough to believe in it. One must work at it."

—ELEANOR ROOSEVELT, SHARED BY JULIE IN MISSOULA, MT

BOULDER

"Ultimately, we have just one moral duty: to reclaim large areas of peace in ourselves, more and more peace, and to reflect it towards others. And the more peace there is in us, the more peace there will be in our troubled world."

—ETTY HILLESUM

PONDER

Peace can be such an abstract concept; it can mean so many things to different people and can shift meaning as contexts change. I've been lately conceptualizing peace as having an internal aspect (serenity within oneself) and an external aspect (harmony between and among beings). I'm increasingly convinced that an important early step in reducing the amount of conflict in the world is to enlarge the quality and quantity of inner peace that is available to us individually.

Finding time for reflection, relaxation, meditation, and/or prayer can strengthen our efforts to cultivate peace in our communities and in our world. As we refine our own ability to calm anxieties, focus attention, and generally center ourselves, we naturally become both more inspired and more effective in addressing interpersonal conflicts. As we are more patient and compassionate with ourselves, we effortlessly extend patience and compassion to others, which expands our ability to listen, to empathize, and to seek mutually beneficial resolutions to the inevitable conflicts that arise in life.

I invite you to join me in refracting peace this week, first by deepening the well of serenity within your own spirit and then making a conscious effort to bring more harmony to those around you.

Peace,
Paul

P.S. I initially described this week's theme as "Reflecting Peace," but that ultimately seemed too passive, like we were supposed to just mirror the peace we encounter. I was eventually energized by the idea of refraction; I imagined light waves of peace transforming as they passed through me and then continuing to spread out and enlighten others. Reflect on it, and if it makes sense to you, refract it as well!

RIPPLES NUMBER 950

Risk Being Seen

PEBBLE

"If I'm going to sing like someone else, then I don't need to sing at all."

—BILLIE HOLIDAY, SHARED BY SARAH IN FOND DU LAC, WI

BOULDER

"Your need for acceptance can make you invisible in this world. Don't let anything stand in the way of the light that shines through this form. Risk being seen in all your glory!"

—JIM CARREY, SHARED BY JUSTIN IN AUSTIN, TX

PONDER

Honeys, I'm home! I'm back from a few weeks of relaxation and rejuvenation and while I thoroughly enjoyed my time away, I am also SO PLEASED to be back online and back to helping create and extend all kinds of Ripples. I hope you are enjoying your summer as well, and I hope that you've been finding ways to play some and rest some and also learn and grow some. And more than anything else, I hope you're allowing the people you encounter to see you and hear you and experience all your glory.

I'm concerned that too many people spend too much time curled up in a ball or withdrawn into the shadows because that seems easier or safer than putting themselves out there. That's understandable, especially since we've all crossed paths with grumpity grumps who've made it their mission to rain on everyone else's parades.

The reality, however, is that hiding away creates challenges and risks as well—it keeps us from moving forward and developing into the fullest, bestest versions of ourselves that the world is counting on. It inhibits our own growth, and it discourages others from developing into their full, best selves as well. They need our help, our encouragement, and our example so that they can risk being seen, too!

I'd love it if we each took some concrete action this week to let ourselves be seen: speaking up in a meeting, telling friends about something you've been working on, or finding some other solid way to share our talents with the world. And if you notice someone else around you doing something to be seen: recognize it, validate them, and applaud their gifts. Those actions will give you a boost as well.

Peace,
Paul

RIPPLES NUMBER 786

Learning to Surf

PEBBLE

"You can't stop the waves, but you can learn how to surf."

—JON KABAT-ZINN, SHARED BY S. ANDERSON IN EDMONTON, AB

BOULDER

"In our lives, change is unavoidable, loss is unavoidable. In the adaptability and ease with which we experience change, lies our happiness and freedom."

—BUDDHA, SHARED BY CARL IN TERRE HAUTE, IN

PONDER

You're pretty awesome sometimes, aren't you? On your best days when everything is going your way—you rock things out in a magnificent way, right? On those days you work hard, you're on top of things, and you're able to bring forth your best self to handle whatever challenges present themselves. And then there are those pesky OTHER days: those days when you aren't feeling it even though (or precisely because) you're facing a crazy mix of deadlines and crises and obstacles that make up your life in that moment. Even really successful people aren't able to bring their best selves to every moment of every day; they sometimes have bad moments, days, weeks, etc.

The trick is to figure out how to activate your "HEY, I KNOW I CAN HANDLE THIS" alert system so when you enter rough waters it takes just a moment to catch your breath before you can surf your way to sanity. Your alert system could be the right music, it could be a pep talk from one of your fierce allies, or perhaps visiting a sacred place that helps you renew your spirit.

Make this week about identifying what activates your "I've got this" button, and then go surf whatever waves of craziness get whipped up in your life.

Peace,
Paul

RIPPLES NUMBER 1049

Delusions of Disconnection

PEBBLE

"There is only one problem and there is only one answer. Every problem emerges from the false belief we are separate from one another, and every answer emerges from the realization we are not."

—MARIANNE WILLIAMSON, SHARED BY TARA IN SALT LAKE CITY, UT

BOULDER

"A human being is a part of a whole, called by us "universe," a part limited in time and space. We experience ourselves, our thoughts and feelings as something separated from the rest; a kind of optical delusion of our consciousness. This delusion is a kind of prison for us, restricting us to our personal desires and to affection for a few persons nearest to us. Our task must be to free ourselves from this prison by widening our circle of compassion to embrace all living creatures and the whole of nature in its beauty."

—ALBERT EINSTEIN, SHARED BY DAVID IN TOPEKA, KS

PONDER

I notice it when I'm driving: I too easily fall into a mindset that all of us are racing each other. So someone who passes me is now winning (which means I'm losing), and if they get in "my" lane too quickly (forcing me to slow down), well I'm sure they did that on purpose because they are meanies. This makes me a dummy for letting them do that to me.

With just a minor tweak of my mindset, I lean into the idea that we are all connected. This shift invites me to step out of the limited game of winners vs. losers or us vs. them, and shift into the LARGER game of life where we're all on the same side because: we are all connected.

This alters my perspective and instead of just focusing on getting ME where I'm trying to go in the most efficient and safest way possible, I began to see that I'm part of an ecosystem of drivers where the ultimate goal is to get us all where we're trying to go in the most efficient and safest way possible. Sure, there are some people who are going "too fast" or "too slow," but once I rev up my patience and generosity even a teensy bit, the drive becomes more enjoyable while only costing an extra minute or two of my time. BONUS POINTS: I get to arrive at my destination a little bit calmer and a little bit happier.

And yes, I regularly encounter people who have forgotten that we are all connected and are careless in our choices. And there are plenty of times that I unwittingly accept their unconscious invitation to compete, which unfortunately causes a chain reaction of unkindness. Luckily, there are also times where I can let it go: instantly and cheerfully accepting that right now they have too much going on in their lives to remember that we are all indeed connected, and we are all here just to help each other find our way home. This gets easier to do when I remember just how many times a day that I am the one who forgets that we are all connected.

Peace,
Paul

RIPPLES NUMBER 876

Becoming Quiet

PEBBLE

"The quieter you become, the more you are able to hear."

—RUMI, SHARED BY ISAAC IN TAMPA, FL

BOULDER

"There is a pervasive form of modern violence to which the idealist most easily succumbs: activism and overwork. The rush and pressure of modern life are a form, perhaps the most common form, of its innate violence. To allow oneself to be carried away by a multitude of conflicting concerns, to surrender to too many demands, to commit oneself to too many projects, to want to help everyone in everything is to succumb to violence. The frenzy of activists destroy the fruitfulness of their work because it kills the root of inner wisdom which makes work fruitful."

—THOMAS MERTON (ADAPTED SLIGHTLY), SHARED BY RENEE, GREEN BAY, WI

PONDER

I concluded a while back that my work in this lifetime is about encouraging us all to more consistently bring our best selves to work, school and life. And let's face it, it's *really* difficult to really show up for anything or anyone when we are depleted. Part of being human is recognizing our limitations and finding the time and courage to build in breaks: quiet time to rest the body, mind, and spirit.

I'm consistently surprised at how sprinkling in a few extra minutes of sleep and/or relaxation time into daily life can improve productivity in a way that more than makes up for the "lost time." I also believe it can be valuable to keep sacred one day each week, or even a solid half day, where work and chores are put on hold for reflection and/or relaxation either by yourself or with loved ones. Beyond daily and weekly rest periods, most top performers I know require occasional extended retreats of solitude to reflect, recharge, and refocus.

If you have been struggling lately to bring your best self to any part of your life, I encourage you to start with a small break, even if it's just a few minutes with calm music and some deep breaths. Remind yourself that you'll be more effective, more generous, and more enjoyable to be around. If you're already getting that done, perhaps you can consider a more substantial break. It won't necessarily be easy to make the time, but won't it be worth it? Try and see.

    Peace,
    Paul

RIPPLES NUMBER 1027

Pain vs. Suffering

PEBBLE

"Pain is a relatively objective, physical phenomenon; suffering is our psychological resistance to what happens. Events may create physical pain, but they do not in themselves create suffering. Resistance creates suffering."

—DAN MILLMAN, SHARED BY LESLIE IN MADISON, WI

BOULDER

"Life provides pain. We provide the suffering. We don't have control over eliminating pain altogether because pain is part of life. There is no pain-free living. We do, however, have at least some control over how we suffer pain. To suffer means to carry, and we are in charge of our way of carrying pain. We learn ways of carrying pain, just like we learn so much else. Some ways we learn are efficient and some are inefficient and even make the pain worse. No, we can't eliminate pain from our lives, but we can suffer or carry pain in a way that doesn't create additional or unnecessary pain. Our challenge is to learn and develop efficient ways to suffer pain."

—DAVID DOANE WRITTEN AND SHARED BY DAVID IN PERRYSBURG, OH

PONDER

There have been a few periods in my life where I didn't realize how attached I had become to pain, unintentionally creating a downward spiral of suffering that made things worse. It isn't that the pain wasn't legitimate. It's just that the pain triggered suffering which then led to more pain. Without realizing it, I was keeping myself from joyful moments that are possible even when pain is present.

Pain does have an upside—it serves as a useful warning alarm for our bodies and our brains. The problem is that it can make it seem like pain is the only thing going on at a given moment. A few months ago, I was struggling with chronic pain that was really bothersome until I happened upon two activities that shifted my perspective and short-circuited the pain-suffering loop.

One activity involved mentally scanning my body to identify the places that had NO pain. It wasn't about ignoring the pain, but instead putting it into context. Noticing all the places I was NOT in pain reminded the system that pain is just one part of what was happening.

I stumbled upon the other activity while grappling with a string of nightly headaches and yet not allowed to take my usual medication. I needed a distraction, so I took myself out to a nice dinner. On the way home, I passed our zoo which was featuring their holiday lights. I wasn't sure whether the crowds and cold and blinking lights would make things better or worse, but I decided to experiment and found it to be a delightful diversion. I was surprised at how much I enjoyed the adventure despite the significant pain.

I hope that the next time you're struggling, you can change your relationship to pain by taking charge of suffering.

Peace,
Paul

RIPPLES NUMBER 753

Here, Now

PEBBLE

"Wherever you are, be all there."

—JIM ELLIOT, SHARED BY MELISSA FROM SAN LUIS OBISBO, CA

BOULDER

"Once you have decided you want the present moment to be your friend, it is up to you to make the first move: Become friendly toward it, welcome it no matter in what disguise it comes, and soon you will see the results. Life becomes friendly toward you; people become helpful, circumstances cooperative. One decision changes your entire reality. But that one decision you have to make again and again until it becomes natural to live in such a way."

—ECKHART TOLLE

PONDER

I hope you recognize the sacred gift that is hidden within today: the possibility of fully embracing the only place and the only time you have to live. Here, Now. What can you do to embrace this particular day in this particular week of your particular life?

Work as hard as you need to, play as much as you can, and be joyfully present through all of it. It won't likely be a PERFECT day, and you may be dealing with some significant challenges. Embrace it all. In fact, pause right now, take three deep breaths and whisper "Here" on the inhale and "Now" on the exhale. I hope that makes a difference today, and I hope YOU make a difference today.

    Peace,
    Paul

P.S. Thank you for reading Ripples today. It really matters to me.

RIPPLES NUMBER 985

Helper's High

PEBBLE

"Shine your light so life is brighter; get a helper's high ... you'll feel lighter."

—MARIE TOOLE, WRITTEN AND SHARED BY MARIE IN DELRAY BEACH, FL

BOULDER

"You cannot get through a single day without having an impact on the world around you. What you do makes a difference, and you have to decide what kind of difference you want to make."

—JANE GOODALL, SHARED BY SCOTT IN MADISON, WI

PONDER

I'm quite confident that most of our regular Ripplers are already well aware of the benefits of unleashing ripples of compassion and kindness. We are the type of folks who figured out a long time ago that doing good for others not only makes karmic sense, it feels good!

Still, it's inevitable that life sometimes gets so full and so stressful that we occasionally drift away from our good intentions of helping others and we forget about the hidden treasures to be found while serving: the perspective shift that comes from seeing the challenges that others are facing; gratitude for the many good things in our own lives that we sometimes take for granted; and the renewed sense of community that grows when we recognize that we're all in this together.

If it has been a while, keep your eyes open for someone who needs a little extra help. If you've been doing a good job of helping others lately, perhaps you can keep your eyes open for someone doing a kind deed and taking a moment to thank them for their efforts. It will compound the helper's high!

Peace,
Paul

P.S. Of course, it's important to remember that there is such a thing as TOO MUCH when it comes to helping others, and we have to keep in mind that without building boundaries and recognizing limits, we put ourselves at risk of compassion fatigue and/or caregiver burnout. Help others in the right amount so your HELPER'S HIGH doesn't cause a crash and burn!

RIPPLES NUMBER 897

The Hero Within

PEBBLE

"I think a hero is any person really intent on making this a better place for all people."

—MAYA ANGELOU, SHARED BY PETE IN SEDONA, AZ

BOULDER

"We live in a world in which we need to share responsibility. It's easy to say, 'It's not my child, not my community, not my world, not my problem.' Then there are those who see the need and respond. I consider those people my heroes."

—FRED ROGERS, SHARED BY JAMIE IN MICHIGAN

PONDER

I spent some time with two of my heroes this weekend: Jason Bourne and Harry Potter. I realize that they are both fictional characters, of course, but having the new Bourne thriller open in movie theaters on the same weekend as the book release of "Harry Potter and the Cursed Child" was an exceptional coincidence and made for a magnificent weekend.

Besides lots of chase scenes and fight scenes, Jason Bourne's adventures focus on the challenges of recovering traumatic memories and deciding how much the darkness in your past defines you and determines your future. Of course, Harry Potter had to face his own troubled past as well, and summon the courage to face demons even when others didn't believe in him.

The plot twists they each face mirror challenges in my own life, and both Jason and Harry have helped me remember how large our internal reserves of courage and strength can be. On our worst days, we tend to forget how powerful we are; on our best days, we forget that unleashing our strengths often inspires others to rise up as well.

I'm going to jump back into reading Harry Potter (don't worry, I promise to #KeepTheSecrets). Meanwhile, I hope you can spend a few minutes this week noticing how much in common you have with your heroes.

Peace,
Paul

RIPPLES NUMBER 868

Imperfectionism

PEBBLE

"Imperfections are not inadequacies; they are reminders that we're all in this together."

—BRENÉ BROWN, SHARED BY STEVE IN WACO, TX

BOULDER

"At the heart of each of us, whatever our imperfections, there exists a silent pulse of perfect rhythm which is absolutely individual and unique, and yet which connects us to everything else."

—GEORGE LEONARD, SHARED BY KELSEY IN FOND DU LAC, WI

PONDER

This week was adventure filled: I fired up some residence life folks just down the street from me at Xavier University and then zoomed out west to spend an evening with the CSU San Bernardino Recreation and Wellness Center Staff. The topics were slightly different, but as usual I included some stories and activities around how to more consistently unleash their best efforts in work, school, and life.

Today's Ripples quotes remind us that there is a difference between trying to bring your best and attempting to be perfect. One requires embracing your strengths and limitations while making a conscious commitment to improvement. The other is an exercise in futility since it demands both hyper-vigilance and an obsessive fear of inevitable errors and omissions.

Striving to be your BEST allows you to keep getting better, while grasping for PERFECTION will always end in defeat. Always. No matter how good you get, no matter how hard you practice: Mistakes. Are. Inevitable. The trick is to embrace your errors as divine gifts: they give you feedback, they help you measure improvement, and they encourage you to cultivate compassion for the imperfect people around you whose mistakes sometimes inconvenience and/or challenge you.

    Peace,
    Paul

"Autumn is a second spring when every leaf is a flower."
—ALBERT CAMUS

autumn

RIPPLES NUMBER 951

Light & Love

PEBBLE

"Do not be dismayed by the brokenness of the world. All things break. And all things can be mended. Not with time, as they say, but with intention. So go. Love intentionally, extravagantly, unconditionally. The broken world waits in darkness for the light that is you."

—L.R. KNOST, SHARED BY PIDGE IN PACIFICA, CA
(who has known me since we were in 5th grade and continues to be a fierce and fabulous friend.)

BOULDER

"Your light is seen, your heart is known, your soul is cherished by more people than you might imagine. If you knew how many others have been touched in wonderful ways by you, you would be astonished. If you knew how many people feel so much for you, you would be shocked. You are far more wonderful than you think you are. Rest with that. Rest easy with that. Breathe again. You are doing fine. More than fine. Better than fine. You're doin' great. So relax. And love yourself today."

—NEALE DONALD WALSCH, SHARED BY REGINA IN GLEN GARDNER, NJ

PONDER

Just when we think the world couldn't get any messier or more troubling, news from North Korea, Venezuela, Charlottesville, and elsewhere proves us wrong. The challenges we're facing are far more complex than many of us are willing to admit, and the potential solutions that will eventually help to improve things will require many people coming together with massive amounts of passion, patience, and persistence. I don't have the answers for how we'll get through this, but I do have confidence that we will.

The steps that we can all take right now to help us move forward involve recognizing and sharing our own reserves of light and love. First, look in the mirror and ponder the compliments that have been shared by people that have told you how important and precious you are to them. Marinate in that light and love. Then look around and identify the people you cross paths with on a regular basis that YOU respect, admire, and/or value. And tell them what they mean to you. Let them marinate in light and love.

If you're feeling especially adventurous, the next step could be to identify some people you *struggle* to respect, admire, and/or value to see if any of them deserve reconsideration. Maybe you haven't sufficiently appreciated how or why their perspective is so different than your own, or you haven't even gotten to know them well enough to understand what their perspective really is all about. At least think about it, and see if you can allow them to marinate in light and love, too.

These might seem like small steps, but small changes in how you think and feel can lead to small changes in your behavior. And it is all of our little actions that can ripple out to change the world.

Sending you Light & Love,
Paul

RIPPLES NUMBER 863

Liking Living

PEBBLE

"I like living. I have sometimes been wildly, despairingly, acutely miserable, racked with sorrow, but through it all I still know quite certainly that just to be alive is a grand thing."

—AGATHA CHRISTIE, SHARED BY SANDY IN MINNEAPOLIS, MN

BOULDER

"One of the most tragic things I know about human nature is that all of us tend to put off living. We are all dreaming of some magical rose garden over the horizon instead of enjoying the roses blooming outside our windows today."

—DALE CARNEGIE, SHARED BY DANA IN SALT LAKE CITY, UT

PONDER

It seems like we are *always* busy. The weekdays are busy with work and school and meetings and practice and go, go, GO! The weekends are just as busy but with different stuff: games and errands and socials and dates and chores and catching up on all the stuff we didn't get done during the week. Our vacations often get crammed with lines and waits and schedules and forced smiles and selfies and such. How many times have you paused in the midst of a massive swirl of overwhelmedness and made a wish or pledged an oath to slow down and savor life? If you're like me, this has happened many, MANY times and is often followed by a brief period of mindfulness and present momentness before the chaotic symphony gradually resumes.

  I don't think the answer is to sequester ourselves in a deep, dark cave of solitude; we'd probably get bored anyway. Instead, I think it is more realistic and more useful to practice embracing the fabulous ups and the challenging downs and even the confusing sidewaysness of our adventures and perhaps create temporary islands of seclusion that briefly allow us to catch our breath before resuming our lives with a bit more calm and a bit more focus.

  Breathe in, breathe out, let go ...

  Peace,
  Paul

RIPPLES NUMBER 1025

The Greatness of Your Smallness

PEBBLE

"The true heroes are more concerned with helping than with advertising their own acts. Become one of them, in the silence of your achievements and the greatness of your smallness."

—JOANNA DE ÂNGELIS, SHARED BY MURILLO IN CHAMPAIGN, IL

BOULDER

"A true hero gets out of bed every morning and goes about life's daily tasks, unnoticed, unassuming and unsung. A true hero takes on responsibility, gives out credit, and always looks for ways to solve a problem. A true hero speaks kindly, acts fairly, endures patiently, enjoys easily. And, facing every day with a simple strength, a true hero persists in the things that matter."

—SOURCE UNKNOWN, SHARED BY DEAR D
(who fervently lives this quote)

PONDER

Fictional superheroes tend to be larger than life and do a magnificent job of inspiring hope and excitement while saving the world over and over again. They help us remember that good can indeed conquer evil, and I value their expansive personas.

In the real world, I believe most of the goodness gets unleashed by everyday heroes who quietly go about their day, making a difference at their jobs and around their community and even in their back yard. These fine human beings make ethical decisions even when they assume no one is watching. They go out of their way to provide assistance when they spot someone in need, and importantly, they are able to extend patience and compassion even when others seem to be running low on reserves of kindness.

While most of them don't need the ego gratification of being in the spotlight, I suspect they do appreciate knowing that their efforts are making a difference and that what they are doing matters. You can tend to the care and feeding of these heroes by keeping your eyes open for great small things and taking the time to deliver a subtle, sincere thank you in the form of head nods, high fives, or perhaps handwritten notes of gratitude.

These small gestures confirm the "greatness of their smallness," and allow these unsung heroes to "persist in the things that matter." Quietly acknowledging their heroism not only will allow you to witness firsthand how good it feels to be validated by others, you'll get a glimpse of how good it feels to deliver that validation. It may seem rather small, but it is indeed pretty great, too!

Peace,
Paul

RIPPLES NUMBER 649

Scare Your Fears

PEBBLE

"Fairy tales are more than true; not because they tell us that dragons exist, but because they tell us that dragons can be beaten."

—G.K. CHESTERTON, SHARED BY ELIZABETH IN LA CROSSE, WI

BOULDER

"I believe that anyone can conquer fear by doing the things he fears to do, provided he keeps doing them until he gets a record of successful experiences behind him."

—ELEANOR ROOSEVELT, SHARED BY ANGIE IN YORK, PA

PONDER

BOO! I thought we could celebrate Halloween today by scaring our fears. Wait now, what? If we take off the mask that our fears wear, we usually find nothing more than an overblown worry about the possible "worst case" outcomes that almost never materialize.

Even in those rare instances when they do come true, they are often less awful than we anticipated. The best way to decrease our fears is to turn on the lights, and in most cases that means taking action. I triple-dog dare you to take some steps today to scare a fear away. If there is an opportunity you have been hesitant to pursue, take some concrete action to start the process. If you have been holding off on having a fierce conversation with someone, maybe you can mentally rehearse the words you want to say, or if you're feeling ready then reach out and set up the time to chat.

And here is the best news: even if it doesn't turn out exactly as you hoped, it will likely make you a braver and wiser person. So, what fear are you going to scare away today?

    Peace,
    Paul

RIPPLES NUMBER 967

The Evolution of Happiness

PEBBLE

"You're not happier because you turn your brain off. You're happier because you encourage yourself to think more deeply about what actually matters."

—CHARLES DUHIGG, SHARED BY HOLLY IN PHOENIX, AZ

BOULDER

"The art of living does not consist of preserving and clinging to a particular mode of happiness, but allowing happiness to change its form without being disappointed by the change; happiness, like a child, must be allowed to grow up."

—CHARLES MORGAN, SHARED BY JOHN IN DENVER, CO

PONDER

Of course we want to be happy. Of course we do! The pursuit of happiness is such a compelling quest that Thomas Jefferson even wrote it into the Declaration of Independence. While I agree that being happy is a worthy outcome of a satisfying life, it's also true that pursuing happiness tends to make a better by-product than a goal in and of itself. This is because the highest level of happiness you'll find by just trying to be happy is a more hedonistic, or pleasure-based type of happiness that tends to be very fleeting: "I'm happy because I have this object or that amount of money or I just ate my favorite food."

Deeper, more sustainable, more meaningful states of happiness are more attainable when we pursue deeper, more sustainable, more meaningful goals. The puzzles and games that keep us entertained and engaged when we are younger no longer hold our attention and eventually lose their magic. As we grow up, we need to find more complicated puzzles and more challenging games to enjoy. Similarly, as we go through (and hopefully grow through) life, the pursuits that have the potential to cultivate and sustain happiness will need to evolve as well.

Give some thought this week to your current and desired levels of happiness. Ask yourself what new actions and thoughts might help you grow into a deeper level of happiness, and what actions and thoughts you might need to graduate from in order to more easily make some changes.

Peace,
Paul

RIPPLES NUMBER 128

Ripples of Experimentation

PEBBLE

"Never be afraid to try something new. Remember that amateurs built the ark. Professionals built the Titanic."

—SOURCE UNKNOWN, SHARED BY LISSA M.

BOULDER

"And I learned what is obvious to a child. That life is simply a collection of little lives, each lived one day at a time. That each day should be spent finding beauty in flowers and poetry and talking to animals. That a day spent with dreaming and sunsets and refreshing breezes cannot be bettered."

—NICHOLAS SPARKS, SHARED BY ELIZABETH R.

PONDER

This week found me in Michigan for an early beginning to the fall series of new-student orientations. The first-year students at Kettering University were exploring the many ways to get involved on campus during the day I visited, and we spent some time encouraging them to experiment with lots of different activities before settling on a few to concentrate more heavily on.

On my way back to the airport in Detroit, I stopped by for dinner with some friends and found that they were doing some experimenting of their own. In the process of baking apple, blueberry, and pumpkin pies for dessert, they discovered they had enough extra dough for a fourth pie ... so they decided to experiment with the leftover ingredients and created a truly unique blueberry/apple pie.

We were all curious to try it, but each of us had our eye on the other pies because we KNEW how delicious they were going to be. It turns out that many of us actually enjoyed the experimental pie the most! Perhaps it was the unique taste, or maybe it was because we didn't know what to expect, but I have decided to spend this week experimenting more.

    Peace,
    Paul

RIPPLES NUMBER 1001

Squeeze and Release

PEBBLE

"These mountains that you are carrying, you were only supposed to climb."

—NAJWA ZEBIAN, SHARED BY ANN IN BREWSTER

BOULDER

"We sometimes resist leaving because we don't want to leave great memories behind. But leaving allows us to embark on new adventures, creating new memories for us to savor. Move on, and you'll enjoy those memories whenever you reminisce."

—MARCUS POWELL WRITTEN AND SHARED BY MARCUS IN IOWA CITY, IA

PONDER

We all have chapters in our lives: various chapters of school, work, relationships, locations, hobbies, etc. And while some of these types of chapters can overlap, it is generally true that each time you start a new chapter in a particular area of your life, the previous chapter comes to an end. Sometimes it's relatively easy to move on to the next thing, but other times can be difficult. Even in transitions where we are excited about the next chapter, we can let feelings of nostalgia and grief keep us from saying goodbye to that which is coming to an end.

A friend of mine is preparing to transition to his next adventure, and yet having a tough time saying goodbye to the previous one. I've been watching from the sidelines, wishing I knew what to say or do to help. It's tough because I've never gone through what he's facing, and I'm not sure exactly what is going through his head and heart as he ponders what is ahead.

Sometimes we're not sure we're ready, or if the timing is right, or if this is what is best for us and possibly others who might be impacted by the transition. When I've been contemplating a big change for myself, I try to keep in mind that I don't need to know EVERYTHING in order to start the new thing, I just have to know enough. And it doesn't have to be precisely the exact best time to start, it just needs to be about the right time. And I don't need to be completely ready, just ready enough. And if I wait until I'm 100% comfortable, I'll likely be waiting forever.

Several nights ago, I woke up thinking about crossing the monkey bars as a kid, and how it takes the right combination of holding on and letting go to make it across to the other side. One hand has to squeeze tight while the other one is releasing. I thought about my friend, wondering if he is in the middle of a double squeeze: not quite ready to let go of the bar he's been hanging onto for a while—which is keeping him from swinging forward to grab the next one. Several times since I had that thought I've noticed my hands are balled into fists and I'm alternately squeezing and releasing.

My wish for him, and my wish for you, is that we all spend a bit of time this week thinking about recent or upcoming transitions, and maybe doing a bit of "squeeze and release" practicing: with our hands, our heads, and our hearts.

Peace,
Paul

RIPPLES NUMBER 886

The Magic of Words

PEBBLE

"Words are, in my not-so-humble opinion, our most inexhaustible source of magic."

—J.K. ROWLING, SHARED BY PABLO IN FT. MYERS, FL

BOULDER

"Your own words are the bricks and mortar of the dreams you want to realize. Behind every word flows energy."

—SONIA CHOQUETTE, SHARED BY JENNIFER AT MARIAN UNIVERSITY, WI

PONDER

Each word we speak matters even if no one else is around to hear it. The words we choose help us identify what we are thinking, encourage us to clarify our feelings, and perhaps most importantly allow us express our intentions which hopefully lead to action. Words are fragrant, and they are potent. (See what I mean?)

When I was in grade school, we explored a series of books to build passion and talent for reading. Each book had a single-word title, and to this day those words unleash magic when I encounter them: Serendipity, Kaleidoscope, Diversity. [I recently found a blog post about them: hmr.posthaven.com] Those books helped me fall in love with words which in turn helped me fall in love with communicating.

Forty years later, one of my most sacred tasks is concocting these weekly splashes. The goal of keeping Ripples short enough to be consumed quickly has fueled my passion for seeking the right words to clearly and concisely transmit an idea. When I nail it, words have the power to cast spells, captivating readers and enticing them to pass it on to others.

Make an extra effort this week to increase both awareness of and mindfulness for the words you and those around you are choosing. If there are words you especially enjoy hearing or speaking, make a conscious decision to see what spells you can cast by using them.

Peace,
Paul

RIPPLES NUMBER 1003

Crazy Powerful

PEBBLE

"There is no excellent beauty that hath not some strangeness in proportion."

—SIR FRANCIS BACON, SHARED BY NATALIE IN CLEAR LAKE, WI

BOULDER

"Don't let what is crazy to them, stop you from creating what is powerful to you."

—AKEEM LLOYD WRITTEN AND SHARED BY AKEEM IN PROVIDENCE, RI

PONDER

A few weeks ago I posted on Facebook my reaction to a heartbreaking poem that popped up in my newsfeed from someone who was struggling mightily. I'd like to share a condensed version of my post for you to ponder:

A long time ago I encountered a boy whose sensitive, not-quite-like-anyone-else spirit was nearly crushed in a world that doesn't value difference. He struggled mightily, but luckily for him (and luckily for the world), he managed to stay alive long enough for his brain and his body to grow into an adulthood that allowed him to heal from some hurts, to make friends with his shadows, and to recognize the differences which made him weird evolved into the distinctions that make him special. He still remembers what it is like to feel impossibly broken, and he remains grateful that he held on long enough to discover just how incredible it feels to find out that you can make a LIVING and make a LIFE while being weird. Because what makes him weird is precisely what makes him special. He still encounters hard times, of course. But he also experiences blissful transcendence, like the times he scrolls his social media feed looking for weary travelers who need to be reminded: everything that helped you make it to today can help you make it a brighter tomorrow.

Hang in there. Rest when necessary, and know that the world needs your kind of crazy. I know this for certain, because you're still here.

Peace,
Paul

RIPPLES NUMBER 1056

The Freedom of Forgiveness

PEBBLE

"To forgive is to set a prisoner free and discover that the prisoner was you."

—LEWIS B. SMEDES, SHARED BY JULIE IN MISSOULA, MT

BOULDER

"If I may, I leave you with this, forgiveness is not about saying what the other person did was okay. It simply means that you choose to no longer suffer when you think about the memory of it. Forgiveness is a gift you give yourself. Forgiveness is freedom."

—LEIGH MORGAN KOECHNER, SHARED BY D IN SAN DIEGO, CA

PONDER

A few months back, I had a meaningful exchange with a fellow Rippler (and fellow Cincinnatian!), Ron Meyer, who shared with me his definition of forgiveness as a quote submission: "The act of freeing yourself of the pain, hurt, isolation, hatred, anger or resentment caused by the words or actions of yourself or another person so that you can increase your capacity to love."

I learned that he had developed this definition of forgiveness while designing a spiritual-growth retreat. Using a great analogy, Ron explained that just as sink drains can build up gunk and reduce the flow of water, there are times when pain, anger, and resentment can build up in our relationships, which in turn reduces the flow of communication and love. Forgiveness, then, can be a form of "spiritual Drano," unclogging our lines of communication, and reducing the barriers to a freer flow of love.

Importantly, Ron also stressed that forgiveness can be a powerful tool for our own physical, mental, emotional and spiritual healing. He wrote, "People tend to miss the point that forgiveness is mostly for us and our own freedom. Forgiveness is not saying that what was done or said was OK. Instead, it is about acknowledging it for what it was and having the courage to let it go so that it does not impact us in a negative way anymore. And forgiveness is not about being weak and giving in, it's about taking back our power and owning our joy."

If you'd like to take more ownership of the joy in your life, it could be useful to spend some time considering past hurts to see if you're ready to experience the freedom of forgiveness.

Peace,
Paul

P.S. Remember that an invitation isn't a command, if this topic doesn't feel ripe for exploration right now, just set it aside or hit delete!

RIPPLES NUMBER 865

Enoughness

PEBBLE

"Be happy with what you have. Be excited about what you want."

—ALAN COHEN, SHARED BY MELINDA IN MADISON, WI

BOULDER

"A life of enough is born in every moment: in the way we listen, the way we respond to the world, the way we see what is and tell the truth of who we are. Every single choice, every single moment, every change of course can bring us closer to a life of peace, contentment, authenticity, and easy sufficiency, a life of being, having, and doing enough."

—WAYNE MULLER, SHARED BY JANE IN IRVINE, CA

PONDER

As many Ripplers prepare to gather with family and/or friends to celebrate Christmas, it's good to recognize the unique mix of joy and anxiety that comes along with giving and receiving gifts. We want others to be surprised and delighted with what is under the tree as much as we want to enjoy the gifts we receive.

And so along with visions of sugarplums, we have plenty of worries swirling in our heads: Have we selected the right gifts? Did we buy enough? Will we get enough? I'm guessing that most of us who are part of Team Ripples have very few unmet NEEDS when it comes to the essentials (food, shelter, clothing) and therefore have the good fortune of spending time and energy contemplating and acquiring our WANTS.

It can be useful to gently remind ourselves and our loved ones that with all the social media-ing and marketing we're exposed to, it's virtually impossible to satisfy our endless cravings for the shiniest objects, newest fashions, and latest gadgets. There's just so much muchness out there to crave! The good news is that we can maximize the magic of this time of year as we mindfully seek the right mix of savoring what we've already received and sharing our bounty with others: family, friends, neighbors, and also those in need whose paths may not cross ours directly but are still a part of our world and deserve a place in our hearts.

When we delight in our Enoughness, unwrapping presents becomes less about what's inside the box and more about what's inside our hearts (which, according to Grinchy legend, has the capacity to grow three sizes in one day!).

Enjoy your holiday, and enjoy your Enoughness!

Peace,
Paul

RIPPLES NUMBER 535

Bubbling Brooks

PEBBLE

"The bubbling brook would lose its song if you removed the rocks."

—SOURCE UNKNOWN, SHARED BY FLORY D., INDIA

BOULDER

"Adversity is like a strong wind. It tears away from us all but the things that cannot be torn, so that we see ourselves as we really are."

—ARTHUR GOLDEN, SHARED BY JAMIE W., MIDDLETON, WI

PONDER

Life is not always easy, eh? I have heard from several fellow Ripplers lately who are experiencing BIG challenges in their lives: loss of loved ones, major disruptions in work/school/life, and dealing with other "stuff" that makes life rocky. It is heartbreaking to hear how difficult life can be for each of us at times. As I look over my responses to them, I notice a common phrase that I have used in various forms. While I try to avoid using absolutes like "always" and "never," I stand by these: Life is not always easy, convenient, pretty, or fair; life, however is ALWAYS worth it.

The hard stuff makes us stronger the same way the heavier weights are what make the difference in strength training. (Many of you have heard me say that I'd do more weight lifting if they weren't so darn heavy. But of course if they were light, they wouldn't help me strengthen my muscles!) Believe me, I have days where I wish all the "rocks" in the bubbling brook of my life could be magically removed. Luckily I have the good sense to remember that so much of my character, my personal strength, and my capacity to help others has grown from dealing with the difficult stuff.

I'm truly sorry if life is extra tough for you right now. I hope you seek good people to support you, calming music to soothe you, and an occasional ice cream or other treat every now and then is pretty darn awesome, too.

    Peace,
    Paul

RIPPLES NUMBER 866

Whimsical Graces

PEBBLE

"Life, with its grinding requirements and whimsical graces, seems to unfold in its own mysterious style and time frame."

—HEIDI PETERSEN, WRITTEN AND SHARED BY HEIDI IN BOULDER, CO
via her annual holiday letter

BOULDER

"Rest in knowing that you are a divine part of What Is. Invite yourself to be a conscious participant in the beautiful and mysterious unfolding without needing to be responsible for it."

—PAT MATSON, WRITTEN AND SHARED BY PAT IN CINCINNATI, OH

PONDER

As we wrap up another year of Ripply adventures, I'm pleased to end the year with the quotes on the opposite page that were written and shared by people I'm lucky enough to know personally. The first quote is from a childhood neighbor-friend who decades ago relocated to a far away land called Boulder, CO. Visiting her family after they moved out there introduced me to my soul's home: the Colorado Rockies. The second quote grew out of a Ripply email exchange with my Cincinnati neighbor-friend and Bruegger's Buddy, Pat, who helped confirm that Cincy should become my new home base.

If your year has been similar to mine, you've faced plenty of "grinding requirements." Hopefully you've also been able to savor the "whimsical graces" that are almost always around even when they are difficult to spot. I suspect that the most satisfying way to say goodbye to the year is to express gratitude for both the delights that made the year special as well as the disappointments that have hopefully generated growth.

Even if you're saying GOOD RIDDANCE to some particularly painful experiences, you can still choose to pause briefly and notice how you're a little stronger and a little wiser because of them. And then, with a wink and a nod the new year will arrive in a few days to provide a fresh batch of experiences, hopefully with a little less grind and a little more whimsy.

See you next year!

Peace,
Paul

Thanks

I'm hesitant to attempt identifying all of our helpers, and I apologize in advance to the kind souls whose names popped into my head moments after this went to press. Still, I want those holding this book to get a glimpse of just how many remarkable people had a hand in unleashing these splashes of inspiration as we share our gratitude...

... To those who helped make Ripples and this book possible ...

Brian Miller asked great questions and offered useful insights that led to the initial creation of the weekly Ripples emails.

Sarah Fisher refined the look of Ripples by providing the right colors, fonts, and vibe.

Leslie Stephany was among our first subscribers, a fantastic quote finder, and in the early years served as our official Kindness Coordinator.

Our Facebook group Team Ripples, especially Diane Kling and Nick Papandria, have helped extend the reach of Ripples to the interwebs.

Patty Craft provided an eagle eye, grammatical gifts, and endless enthusiasm for this project.

Clare Finney brought beauty and grace to the layout and design of this book.

My sweetie, Jamie Markle, rose early to read a dozen Ripples every day for months and months (and months!), yet still had enough sanity to bring to this project his sharp editorial eye and vast experience in publishment (and who may or may not allow this word to be printed). Oh, and he bakes the most delicious oatmeal chocolate chip cookies. Ever.

... And to those who provided immeasurable support over the years ...

Bridget Kesner, Meg Dutnell, Sarah Hhundt, Terri Potter, and Su Cary (hey, sis!) were extremely helpful in providing early and ongoing opportunities for me to unleash ripples in multiple organizations.

Maura Cullen, Paul Smith, Diane Hamilton, Colene Elridge, Toby Causby, Pidge Meade, and Mary Anne em Radmacher have thoroughly demonstrated that mentoring and friendship can indeed go hand in hand.

My higher education peeps have helped unleash countless ripples throughout campus recreation (NIRSA), orientation (NODA), residence life (NACURH), and at hundreds of colleges and universities that have invited me to make a splash on their campuses—a special shout out to Cal Poly (Cal Pauly loves you!) and Central Michigan (Fire up, Safari Chips!).

Ripples have also found their way into K-12 education, parks and recreation, healthcare, nonprofits, and more than a few businesses (over 10% of our Ripplers are P&Gers!). Oh, and so many credit unions let me hang out with them on MLK Day, Presidents' Day, Columbus Day, & Veterans Day.

My aunts, Sisters Miriam and Florence Wesselmann, helped me fall in love with words and helped me fall in love with myself. Their boundless enthusiasm and curiosity affirmed my twin destinies as an educator and lifelong learner.

And finally, Ron Becker has been a solid (and stoic) source of advice, support, and friendship for 25 years.

Copyright © 2019 Paul Wesselmann

All rights reserved. No portion of this book may be reproduced—mechanically, electronically, or by any means, including photocopying—without written permission of the publisher.

It is our intent and sincere hope that all of the words of wisdom shared in these pages have proper attribution and permissions. We apologize for any errors and encourage you to contact us via UnleashRipples.com to share any concerns.

Back cover photo © Helen Adams
Cover and interior design by Clare Finney
Edited by Jamie Markle

Library of Congress Cataloging-in-Publication Data is available.

ISBN 978-1-7340995-6-0

Printed in the United States of America

First printing December 2019
10 9 8 7 6 5 4 3 2 1

ABOUT THE AUTHOR

Paul Wesselmann is a writer, educator, and speaker with a passion for empowering and uplifting others by unleashing ripples of positivity and growth. Paul holds degrees in psychology and higher education and has spent more than two decades traveling around North America as a leadership trainer and keynote speaker. His newsletter, Ripples, is read by more than 30,000 subscribers every Monday morning, and by many more who follow @RipplesGuy on just about every social media platform. Paul lives in Cincinnati, Ohio, visits the Colorado Rockies frequently, and believes that effective living includes proper amounts of meditation, exercise, rest, and angel food cake.

ABOUT THE EDITOR

Jamie Markle is an author, artist, and book editor with more than 20 years of experience in publishing. Jamie is the author of nine books, including five books in the *AcrylicWorks: The Best of Acrylic Painting* series. Jamie holds a degree in Fine Art from Xavier University, where he studied painting and drawing. In addition to making art, gardening, and writing, he enjoys indulging his sweet tooth, which he counteracts by running six days a week. He spends his free time working on the 100-year-old home and garden that he shares with Paul in Cincinnati, Ohio.

Join the Ripples Community!

Sign up to receive our weekly Ripples emails:
UnleashRipples.com

Join Team Ripples on Facebook:
Facebook.com/groups/TeamRipples/

Follow @RipplesGuy on
Instagram, Pinterest, Twitter, and LinkedIn

Receive a random splash of inspiration any time you need one:
2Rpl.me

Learn how Paul can fire up your organization:
TheRipplesGuy.com